What Girls Say

Tell It Like It Is

What Boys Say

What Girls Say
Tell It Like It Is
What Boys Say

By Karle Dickerson

SCHOLASTIC INC.
New York Toronto London Auckland Sydney
Mexico City New Delhi Hong Kong

ISBN 0-439-16114-2

Cover and interior design by Louise Bova

Published by Scholastic Inc., 555 Broadway,
New York, NY 10012.

12 11 10 9 8 7 6 5 4 0 1 2 3 4 5/0

Printed in the U.S.A. 01
First Scholastic printing, January 2000

Contents

What Girls Say

Tell It Like It Is

What Boys Say

Intro

Three Boys and Three Girls

It's not always easy trying to figure out other kids. No doubt you've often wondered about what makes them tick. Maybe it's when you spot a group of 'em giggling together in a school hallway — and you wonder what they find sooo funny. Or when you're talking to someone who seems to be beyond cool, and you can't help thinking . . . does this person have a secret dread of being alone in dark places? Or perhaps it's when you're cruising the shopping mall, and there's a group of boys giving each other these . . . looks. You find yourself wondering why and trying to guess — yet again! — what's going on. Hmmm, you think, these boys are around my age, so I oughta be able to guess what they're up to. But I've got no clue. What's up with the way they act anyway?

Are you ready to meet new girls? Are you ready to meet new boys? We were interested too, so we took the time to hang with some cool kids and got to know what's on their minds. We selected six kids (three girls, three boys) with a range of personalities — the kind of kids you'd probably like to know —

and spent countless hours listening one-on-one while they talked and talked. (And *did* they talk!)

We traveled to their hangouts, like the mall, athletic fields, skateboard sites, their homes, and swimming pools, and asked questions. Then we sat back and listened. We continued to chat on the phone, via e-mail, and even snail mail to give you the scoop on what's going on in their world. So check out what these kids have to say about everything on their minds from their friends, family, and pets, to school, time alone, and much, much more! You'll get a jump-start on knowing more about what's what with girls — and figure out some of those whys about guys.

First, you'll want to meet the kids.

Lexy, age 11: She's the fun-loving type who knows the real deal — and isn't afraid to say it. Friendly (with a capital "F"!), Lexy is full of energy. She's petite and blond with a big smile and laughing blue eyes. An enthusiastic soccer player, she loves stuffed animals and likes people who go out of their way to treat others right.

Devon, age 12: This all-around girl doesn't hesitate to let others know who she is. It's not that she's bossy about anything. It's just that when you're having a convo with her, you know where she stands. Her opinions are strong and her deep brown eyes don't miss much. If things get tough, she falls back on humor to see her through. She has sandy blond shoulder-length hair that she likes to style in a zillion different ways. She prides herself on being in shape, and you can usually find her in some sort of sports uniform, since she spends most of her spare time at one sort of athletic event or another.

Chrissy, age 10: No doubt about it, this is a multidimensional girl. She's outgoing but has quiet moments where she loves nothing more than to curl up with a good book. Her brown eyes are dreamy and framed by dark brunette hair that's thick and full. While she's not a sports nut (she seems to prefer board games and card games), she does occasionally like to step up to the softball plate and get a hit for her team. She's the kind of girl who definitely puts family first, but she still makes sure she has time for her friends.

Travis, age 12: Devon's first cousin, Travis is the kind of guy you'd like to call a close pal because he's easy to talk to and his happy grin is infectious and inviting. Built compactly, he's got dark blond spiked hair and clear blue eyes. He's the first to help a friend in need, and he knows just what to say to boost your spirits and lift you out of blahdom. But you'll want him around when you're feeling upbeat as well. He's the guy you look to when you want a special friend to turn up the volume on a party and crank up the good times.

Andrew, age 11: You don't have to look hard to find this sports-minded guy. Wherever there's a grassy field and a soccer net, you'll be sure to spot him. He's the well-muscled, light-brown-haired guy who seems to be goofing around a little, but he actually demands the best of himself. You can tell he pays attention to his appearance. His hair is rarely out of place and he wears the latest style of clothes with care. When you first meet him, you can't help but smile at his playful ways.

Tino, age 10: This thoughtful guy greets you with a steady gaze from his deep, dark brown eyes. One look, and you can tell he's sensitive and caring. His dark, almost-black hair is combed back and slicked down. Powerfully built and on the tall side, he seems destined for success. He doesn't talk loudly or forcefully, but you figure out in a hurry that he knows what's right and what's wrong—and he's pretty clear on the way things ought to be. No wonder other kids turn to him for advice.

Chapter One

The Real You

"What are some adjectives you'd use to describe yourself?"

Lexy: Wow, that's hard. I'd say I'm athletic because I like lots of sports. Sometimes I can be shy, but mostly with people I don't know that well. I'm nice. I try to avoid arguments and hurting people's feelings. Most of all, I'm happy. I have a nice life, a good family, and friends. How could I not be happy?

Devon: I'd say I'm humorous. I always look for the funny side of a sad or boring situation. I'm pretty confident. I know my own style, what I'm good at and what I'm not good at. I think I'm kind. I can't stand seeing someone cry and I always try to make people feel better.

Chrissy: I think I'm kinda shy at times. It's hard for me when I meet new people. It's hard to know what to say, but after a while, I can talk with them. Also, I'd use the word active to describe myself. I've always gotta be going or working, or creating something.

Travis: I would use the words friendly and outgoing. I like having lots of friends, so I go out of my way to talk to people and get to know them. And it's not just kids, either. I can talk to adults pretty easily, too. Also, I'd say I'm the kind of kid who stands out. Maybe it's because I find it easy to go up and start conversations so people notice me.

Andrew: I guess nice would describe me. I try to consider other people's feelings and do and say things that don't hurt others. I'm pretty cool, I guess. Another adjective? Athletic. Definitely athletic.

Tino: Shy, especially when I meet new people. Since I don't know them, I never know what to talk about that would interest them, so I just kind of stand there and say nothing for a while.

Karle: ***Who doesn't feel shy sometimes?! It seems to be a universal feeling.***

"Under which situations do you feel most confident?"

Lexy: I feel sooo ready when I'm asked to run my fastest, say at a playground or track meet. I never have a second thought. I just know I can kick in with the speed. It feels good to know I'm good at something like that.

Devon: I feel most confident when I'm around good friends whom I really trust. It's a great feeling not to worry about anything and concentrate only on exchanging ideas and having fun.

Chrissy: I am a planner, and when someone asks me to plan something, I know I'm the one for the job. It doesn't matter what it is. If it's a matter of putting together a list of things that need to be done and thinking something through, I know I can do it.

Travis: I think for me it's when a friend needs cheering up. I just know if I go over and try to offer a little sympathy and a listening ear that I'll succeed in lifting that person's spirits. I like being capable of doing something like that that's important for someone else.

Andrew: I feel most confident when I am about to take a penalty kick in soccer. It doesn't matter how big or important that particular game is. Like if it means winning a championship or winning a tournament, I don't even worry for a second that I might not be able to do it. Even if everyone's eyes are on me, I just know I'll make that kick.

Tino: When someone asks me to score for the kickball team, I know I can do it.

"What do you dream of doing or being one day and why?"

Lexy: I really want to be an artist because I love to paint. I like to work in acrylics the best. I keep my favorite paintings bundled together under my bed. My parents have framed a few of my pictures. I think it would be fun to go to art school one day.

Devon: I'd like to be an architect or interior designer. I am really interested in cool buildings and interesting houses. Usually when people go places, they will walk along the streets and look into store windows. I look up above the windows and see how the buildings are designed. I like to tag along when my parents go to those home improvement stores and look at all the tiles and stuff. It's fun to imagine designing a room. As a designer, you also get to meet a lot of people.

Chrissy: My best friend and I plan to open a beauty parlor. We both love doing hair, makeup, and nails. I like trying different hairstyles, experimenting with makeup, and painting nail designs. I think it would be a fun career, and you could try out even more styles because you'd have so many people to work on.

Travis: No question about it, I want to be a pro surfer. I'd love to do that all day long instead of having to have a job in an office. It's the best feeling in the world to stand up on your longboard and just ride. That would be so cool to get paid to do that. Maybe I could even open a surfing school and teach other people how to surf.

Andrew: I want to do lots of things. I'd like to be a surfer, a pro soccer player, and a pediatrician. I love to surf and play soccer, and I like kids. So at this point, I can't really decide because there are so many things I want to do.

Tino: I'd like to be a fighter pilot because I am really into fighter jets. It would be great to wake up each day knowing I was going to be flying my own jet. I can't think of anything I'd rather do more than fly for a living.

"What is your favorite possession?"

Lexy: I am sooo attached to my stuffed bear, Rumples. I've had him since I was 7 years old. He's so cute. I take him with me when we go on family vacations, so he's traveled a lot.

Devon: My teddy bear, what else? I've had him since I was 3, and he's been in the wash a zillion times. Once he got lost at a hotel. I left him in the bed, and the housekeepers swept him up in the sheets. We had to save him from those huge hotel laundry bins. I was so scared we wouldn't find him. He's kind of flat, so I call him Pancake. My cousin thinks he's so mashed up, I should call him Roadkill!

Chrissy: I have three things. I have a stuffed dog and doll my grandmas gave me. Both of my grandmas have passed away, so these things are super-special to me. Also, I have this stuffed horse that I really like. I saved up to buy him with my own money, and that makes him pretty special.

Travis: My favorite possession is my surfboard. I bought it from this vintage surf shop, and it's kind of scuffed up from being used so much. When I bring it out on the beach, all the kids want to know where I got it because their boards are all shiny and new—not as cool as mine.

Andrew: I have this trophy that I won in a tournament. It's special to me because my team and I worked so hard to earn it. We had to play a zillion teams and beat them all. We were getting tired because it was a multi-day tournament, but we didn't let up. It has a special place on the shelf by my bed.

Tino: I can't live without my Nintendo. I could play it for hours and forget about everything else. Unfortunately, my parents limit the amount of time I can play on it, so the times I can play mean even more to me.

> **Karle:** *What's with girls? Their fave stuff is cuddly. What's with boys? Their fave stuff is anything but cuddly!*

"What do you like about your appearance?"

Lexy: I like my hair because it's not too short and not too long, so it's easy to brush. I just had it cut the perfect length where it's not too much hassle to take care of, but I can still tie it back in a ponytail if I need to, to get it out of the way.

Devon: I like my hair color, which is sun-streaky blond, and the way it looks with my brown eyes. Lots of people compliment me on the combination because most blonds have green or blue eyes.

Chrissy: I like my hair because it's thick and shiny. I don't have to condition it that often because it's healthy. My friends play with my hair and like to braid it because it's so thick.

Travis: I like my eyes, I guess. The color's OK, and I think my eyes look happy.

Andrew: I like the way I dress. Of all the things about my appearance, that's the thing I like the most.

Tino: I like my hair because of the way it's cut. I finally got a cut I really like after a few years of having these cuts that just didn't work that well.

Karle: *Hmmm. Hair seems to be a big thing with girls–at least with these girls–and even with one of these boys! How do you rate your hair?*

"What bugs you most about your appearance?"

Lexy: There's this weird red dot under my eye that sometimes seems to disappear. Then when I least expect it, it seems to be redder than ever. I don't know what it is, but whenever I glimpse it in the mirror, I freak. I can't stand it.

Devon: I have a bunch of scars on my legs, mostly from sports and falling down on the playground. I don't let the scars stop me from wearing shorts in the summer or anything, but I sure wish they'd go away. I look like I've been in battle.

Chrissy: Sometimes my weight bugs me. I just wish I could find the right weight that suits me.

Travis: My hair bothers me. At times, I want it to go one way, and it goes the other. I can't figure it out. It doesn't matter if I get it wet again and try to comb it another way, it just won't do what I want it to. It drives me insane some days when I want to look good.

Andrew: Nothing bugs me about my appearance.

Karle: *Lucky Andrew!*

Tino: I wish I were taller. I'm tall enough, I guess. But I sure hope I grow to be even taller. I don't want to end up being short.

"When does your self-esteem tend to take a nosedive?"

Lexy: My self-esteem really sinks low when I mess up on a test. My schoolwork is important to me, and when I get a low grade, I feel my confidence go into total wobble mode.

Devon: When I have a bad day at a sports practice, I don't need a coach to tell me that I'm not performing. There's this tape that runs in my head that says, "Whoa, did you ever whiff that ball," or "Nice miss you just had, Devon." I go over and over my mistakes and feel unsure of myself for a few hours afterward.

Chrissy: I feel my self-esteem plunging when kids tease me. It's not that I think they're right, or that there's something wrong with me. It's that I'm unsure as to how to stop them from going at me.

Travis: When friends are counting on me to go with them or be somewhere and for some reason I can't go, I feel my confidence plunge, knowing that I let them down. I don't like to disappoint people after I've said I'd do something.

Andrew: When I'm around certain friends who think they're incredibly great at everything they do, I sometimes feel unsure of myself. I won't really speak up or do anything that might draw attention to myself at those times.

Tino: When a teacher or coach asks me to run a mile, I can feel my self-esteem sink to my toes. I hate running for that long of a distance because I know I just can't hack it if I'm not in shape.

> **Karle:** *You can't expect to have it totally together all the time! Everyone loses their confidence sometimes.*

"When do you feel most nervous?"

Lexy: I get totally nervous before a big soccer game. I feel all jumpy and I don't want people to talk to me. I can't eat anything either, which is a loser, because you need to eat before a game or you don't have any energy.

Devon: I get nervous before big games too. Like last summer when our softball team was going for the Little League World Series spot, my stomach was doing these incredible wheelies. I'd keep walking back and forth in the dugout before it was my turn to bat and my teammates kept yelling at me to sit down. I think I was making them even more nervous.

Chrissy: My most nerve-wracking time is when I've got to stand up and speak in front of people. Like in class when the teacher makes us give a report or something. I can't stand it. I just want to run away.

Travis: I think it's when I've done something wrong and I'm trying to figure out if my parents already know or if I should just confess. I watch them and look for clues that they're mad at me and just waiting for the perfect opportunity to bring it up. I feel all tense guessing. I'll imagine over and over telling them what I've done wrong and try to guess what their reaction will be. I should just get it over with, I suppose, and just tell.

Andrew: It's when I'm about to go down a hill in a humungous roller coaster. You know, just as you're at the top and the roller coaster pauses for a second, but it feels like practically forever. You feel your stomach roll up into your throat. You can't breathe and you feel like your heart has stopped beating.

Tino: I get nervous about meeting someone new. I can't talk, and I have trouble looking at that person. I find myself wishing I was a billion miles away.

"When do you feel most angry?"

Lexy: I feel angry when someone takes something of mine without asking. It doesn't matter if it's a big or little thing. Like if someone snags a pencil at school without permission, it annoys me. I mean, why couldn't they ask? I don't mind lending stuff, but I hate people just taking.

Devon: I get most angry when someone I thought was my friend hurts me on purpose. It's one thing when an enemy does something mean. You're not surprised. But when it's a person who acts like she's on your side, then she does something crummy and seems to like the fact that she hurt your feelings, I just want to scream.

Chrissy: I get really mad when people make fun of me. I have to take deep breaths and walk away because I really want to yell at them so loudly!

Travis: I am sooo angry when I'm fighting with people, whether it's my friends, enemies, or family. I don't know what it is, but when someone starts an argument with me, I just feel all shaky and I boil inside. Sometimes I lose my temper. I can't help it.

Karle: ***Whoa there, Travis! Count to 10.***

Andrew: I guess it's when my older brother — he's 17 — starts picking on me. I just want to beat him up. When other people do stuff like that, it doesn't bother me as much, but when it's him, I can't stand it.

Tino: I get angry when someone blames me for something unfairly. It seems like I can't really defend myself. Like the more I say I didn't do it, the more people around probably think I did do it. And if I say nothing, it really looks like I did something. It's the worst when there's nothing you can do.

"What do you worry about?"

Lexy: I worry about being stung by bees. It hurts so much to be stung. Whenever I see one buzzing around the lunch tables at school or around my feet at camp, I can't help screaming and running. I know some people think that makes me a wimp, but I just can't handle bee stings.

Devon: Even though it's a long way off, I worry about going to high school. My older brother is in high school, and it seems hard. I guess by the time I get there, I'll know what to do because I'll be older. But right now, it seems like the work is impossible. I look at his textbooks sometimes, and they seem like they're written in another language.

Chrissy: I don't know exactly why, but I worry about dying. Sometimes I wake up in the night, and my heart is pounding because I start to think about it.

Travis: I kind of worry about one day not understanding my schoolwork and failing all my classes. I have this mental picture of just opening a book one day and not getting it at all.

Andrew: I worry about fire. I sometimes drive past a fire engine or a house that's burned down, and I start thinking about it. I imagine fire burning down my house and try to figure out what I'd try to save.

Tino: I know it's weird, but I worry about aliens landing on Earth. I figure they're probably out there, so what's to keep them from coming here one day? That would be so scary.

Karle: *Well, it seems like everyone worries about stuff. The trick is to not let it get to you and stop you from having fun.*

"What was your most humiliating moment ever?"

Lexy: One time in gym class, we were in the girls' locker room. The girls started goofing around and pantsed me. That was bad enough, but what made it worse was that I was wearing these old *Aladdin* undies I dug up from the bottom of my drawer because everything else was in the laundry. This one girl yelled, "Lookit! She's wearing *Aladdin* underwear!" Everyone was laughing themselves sick, and I wanted to absolutely die or at least disappear into the locker room floor. I couldn't do anything but tell them to just shut up.

Devon: I think it was when my violin teacher excused me and this other girl from performing in the school musical. He was nice about it and said he just didn't need so many players, but everyone in the class knew it was because we just weren't that good as violinists. This one nasty girl who thinks she's such a hot violinist gave us these snarky looks, which we pretended not to see. After class, we laughed about it, but I was secretly embarrassed.

Chrissy: It was the time when my teacher yelled at me in front of the whole class for something I didn't even do. I could feel my cheeks get all hot. I couldn't even tell her I didn't do it because the teacher was blabbing on and on about what a creepy thing it was for me to do. She wouldn't listen to a word I tried to say. What a jerk. I was so humiliated.

Travis: It was when I was 4, and I loved *The Little Mermaid* video. When my mom asked me what I wanted to do for my birthday, I said I wanted a little mermaid party. When the kids from my preschool came over, they teased me. They were into Ninja Turtles and your basic boy stuff. That was the first time I realized how people judged you and tried to tease you into liking only what they liked.

Andrew: Once, during this really important soccer game, I went for a big kick. Everyone was watching me, and I kicked, missed, and fell with a huge thump onto the grass. People were laughing. I was humiliated, but I laughed too to cover up how I was really feeling. People came up and teased me afterward.

Tino: I played with my older sister's toys when I was really little, and when my friends saw me, they teased me nonstop. I had to pretend not to like her toys and made sure not to let anyone see me if I ever played with them again.

Karle: ***Everyone has (and remembers) embarrassing moments. What's your most embarrassing moment?***

"What are your favorite kinds of parties?"

Lexy: My favorite parties are roller-skating parties. We go to the local rink and rent skates. I really like to skate with my friends. It's nice to talk with them as we go around and play games on our skates. Sometimes, when the rink people take song requests and turn up the music, we dance skate to our favorite tunes. That's so much fun.

Devon: I love sleepovers with my pals from school. We crank up our CDs and talk and munch. Sometimes we do lip-synching or makeovers where we give each other really weird hairdos. My favorite times are when we talk all night and act goofy.

Chrissy: I like sleepovers, especially with my friends Anna, Jackie, and Sasha. We huddle under the covers and have the biggest gabfests.

Travis: My favorite parties are the kind where I just call up a few friends and they come over right away. We don't plan anything. We don't do anything special; we just hang out. Sometimes we eat pizza and flop around someone's swimming pool.

Andrew: I like parties where we go miniature golfing. The best ones are the ones where my friends from school and I can golf together. We like to get all competitive and see who's got the best score.

Tino: The best parties are the ones held at video arcades. The more classmates that can be there, the better. We can spend hours playing video games.

"What are some of your favorite books?"

Lexy: I love fantasies, books about things that could never happen in real life. It's fun to read about stuff that you can only picture in your imagination because the rest of the time, you have to live in the real world.

Devon: I like any books that are first-person, and the narrator is a girl my age. It's interesting to see what she thinks about and whether she has the same feelings as I do.

Chrissy: I like books about groups of friends, especially series. It's fun to see the friends having different adventures and getting stuck in situations. I like to guess how they're going to get themselves out of the messes at the end.

Travis: I enjoy mysteries. I like to figure out who did the bad thing and see if I was right. It's like a puzzle, putting the clues together.

All-Time Favorite Reads

Lexy: *I loved that little kids' book* Goodnight Moon.

Devon: *I really like reading* Chicken Soup for the Kid's Soul.

Chrissy: *I like the* Babysitters' Club *series.*

Travis: *I like* The Pigman.

Andrew: Soccer Halfback, *by Matt Christopher.*

Tino: *It's called* The Scary Story Reader.

Andrew: I think any books about sports are my favorites. I like the parts where the authors really describe game strategies, especially if they know what they're talking about.

Tino: I read either mystery or horror books. I like suspense, and I like to be scared a little. Sometimes when I read a scary book late at night, it gives me the creeps.

* * *

"What kind of music do you listen to?"

Lexy: Lots of kids don't like it, but I really like jazz. It calms me down and I can do other things while I listen to it.

Devon: I listen to a big variety, including soft pop and classical. I clean my room while listening to music and it makes the work go faster.

Chrissy: I listen to Christian rock and pop because it's easy to listen to.

Travis: My favorite music is alternative. I like all kinds of music, but I always seem to come back to alternative. I don't know why.

Andrew: I like punk. The louder the better!

Tino: Rap. Definitely rap. I just like the beat.

All-Time Favorite Songs

Lexy: "You Were Meant for Me," *by Jewel.*

Devon: "I Will Remember You," *by Sarah MacLachlan.*

Chrissy: "Oh, No, What Are We Going to Do?" *from Veggie Tales.*

Travis: "Pretty Fly for a White Guy," *by Offspring.*

Andrew: "What's My Age Again?" *by Blink 182.*

Tino: "Look Into My Eyes," *by Bone Thugs 'n Harmony.*

All-Time Favorite Movies

Lexy: *Poochie*

Devon: *Stepmom*

Chrissy: *The Parent Trap*

Travis: *Austin Powers*

Andrew: *Big Daddy*

Tino: *The Lost World, Jurassic Park*

"What kinds of movies do you prefer?"

Lexy: I like those basic G-rated movies. They're just fun and light and they don't make me get into bad moods. Oh, yeah, occasionally I like scary movies too. But not too scary.

Devon: I like comedies because I like to laugh and not have to think too hard. I mean, I think at school, so when I'm having fun, I just want to kick back and laugh.

Chrissy: It doesn't really matter to me what kind they are. I like most movies.

Travis: Depends on who I'm with. If it's just me, I like horror or drama. But if I'm with a group, I like comedy. It's better when you're with lots of people to pick a movie that everyone will like, which is usually a comedy.

Andrew: I like a wide range, from comedy to action to horror. Depends what kind of mood I'm in, or if there's something showing at the theater that I've heard about and specifically want to see.

Tino: Science fiction is my favorite.

Fave TV Shows

Lexy: *I really like cartoons like* "Pokémon."

Devon: *I like all kinds, even reruns like* "The Wonder Years."

Chrissy: *I like any of the shows on* Nickelodeon.

Travis: *I like sitcoms like* "Home Improvement." *I wish it hadn't ended its run.*

Andrew: *I like comedy and action, and I like* "The Simpsons."

Tino: *I like the* History Channel *or cartoons for times when I just want to veg out a little bit.*

Three Favorite Foods

Lexy: *Pizza, chocolate, and toast*

Devon: *Tacos, crackers and cheese, bananas and peanut butter*

Chrissy: *Tacos, pizza, and spaetzel with gravy*

Travis: *Enchiladas, pizza, and steak*

Andrew: *Pizza, cookies-and-cream ice cream, and cherry Popsicles*

Tino: *Chinese food, pizza, hamburgers*

Karle: *Hmmm . . . so 5 out of 6 kids recommend pizza as the food of choice!*

Chapter Two

A Few of My Favorite Things

"What are your hobbies?"

Lexy: I like making things with beads. I have all these pretty beads I've collected and when I have time, I like to sit and create really colorful necklaces. They're fun to wear, and people always ask me where I bought them. I like making them for friends. Also, I collect Pokémon cards. I have a huge collection.

Devon: My hobbies are my sports. I really like playing all kinds including travel softball, club volleyball, and club soccer. Another hobby I have is volunteering with this group I belong to.

Chrissy: I like doing crafts, all kinds of them. I especially like doing things with stickers. I like collecting them and making games with them. One time I pretended to have a travel agency and I used the plane and train stickers to decorate the pages with my "customers'" travel plans.

Travis: My favorite hobbies are skateboarding and surfing. Mostly I skateboard because I can't get to the beach all the time. I have this great board that I do tricks on, like grinding and jumping. I practice whenever I can.

Andrew: My hobby is collecting Pez dispensers. I have all kinds including Looney Tunes, Garfield, and Halloween-themed dispensers.

Tino: My hobbies are playing soccer and football. Anytime I can, I try to round up a group of friends to play. If I can't find anyone who's free to play, I practice handling the ball by myself.

* * *

"You have an hour of free time. What would you most likely do?"

Lexy: I'd most likely eat some kind of snack food and watch TV — whatever's on — or read if I'm in the middle of a really good book.

Devon: I'd play outside with my 2-year-old brother or write letters to friends. I have lots of pen pals from the sports camps I've been to, so I'd use the time to catch up with them, maybe by e-mail.

Chrissy: In the summer I'd swim. Other times I'd read.

Travis: I'd invite a friend over. We'd watch TV, listen to music, or goof around on our skateboards.

Andrew: I'd most likely go to my friend Ryan's house and see if we could figure out something to do over there. If the day's warm, we might walk to the beach and just sit around and let the time drift by.

Tino: I'd grab some of my friends and go play outside.

***

"How do you beat boredom?"

Lexy: I know it sounds weird, but when I'm really bored, I clean my room. It's always incredibly messy, and anyway, if I don't have anything to do, I might as well clean it a little. Sometimes I find something that I'd lost for a long time and that makes the work worth it.

Devon: I'll call up friends on the phone and talk. But I have to be really bored because it's not as much fun to talk on the phone as it is to go to their houses and see them in person.

Chrissy: I'll make something. I'll pull out my

stickers and markers and sort through them, or maybe create something.

Travis: If there's nothing else to do, I'll go hang with my 6-year-old brother. We'll play with our animals. We take the bunnies out of their cages and let them run around the house—until my mom gets mad. Sometimes we'll play hide-and-seek or I'll make up monster games to play with my little bro. He loves those games.

Andrew: I'll watch TV. If there's nothing good on, I'll just sit there and channel surf. If it's really bad, I'll go listen to my CDs for a while.

Tino: If I really get bored, I read a book.

"Where is your favorite place to be by yourself?"

Lexy: My favorite place to go is my room. I like to close the door and just flop on my bed. It's nice to be surrounded by my stuff and be able to do whatever I want.

Devon: I go to summer camp in Michigan, and there's a bridge over a stream called Turtle Bridge where you can watch the turtles. It's sooo peaceful, and I just love daydreaming there.

Chrissy: Where else? My room. It's so relaxing, I just climb onto my bed and read. Even though I share my room with my sister, I feel so calm when I'm in it, I can get lost in my book and not hear any noise or distractions.

Travis: I like to be at the beach. I don't care if it's winter or summer. It's cool to walk along just at the water's edge and feel the sand on your feet and think about stuff.

Andrew: I like to hang out in my room, blocking out the world and listening to my music.

Tino: I go to the living room when no one else is there. It's nice to have the whole room to myself.

Karle: ***Do you also like hanging out in your room the best?***

"Describe your bedroom."

Lexy: It's mostly light green. I have a green-and-white comforter on my bed which is piled high with stuffed animals. I have a big rug with an abstract chicken on it, a weird painting of a psycho bunny that a friend of my mom's made, and a few posters.

Devon: It's got a light blue carpet, cheery yellow walls, and yellow-and-blue plaid curtains. It's pretty organized, even though it's jammed with books, trophies, and my stuffed animals. I have lots of framed pictures of my friends everywhere. My room is happy because it's so alive with good memories.

Chrissy: I share my room with my little sister, Jordan. She has a twin bed, and I have a full-sized bed. I have a bookshelf for a headboard and a brown dresser. My room is the most comfortable place in the world.

Travis: It's done with a Route 66 theme, so there are cars everywhere — on the curtains, and on my comforter, and there are models of classic cars on my shelves.

Andrew: It's filled with soccer trophies, books, my TV, and my radio. My sports stuff is everywhere. There are athletic bags tossed around. My longboard and golf bag are propped against the wall.

Tino: I've got my Pokémon stickers and cards piled around my bed. My model planes are everywhere. The room's basically silver and green.

"What's your favorite thing in your room?"

Lexy: Definitely my stuffed animal collection. I've been collecting them for years. They're on my bed and on shelves and everywhere.

Devon: A picture frame shaped like a chair and a bucket of fabric daisies. The frame holds a picture of my friends and me with our arms around each other. We're laughing and having fun.

Chrissy: My bed. It's a full-sized bed and it's huge. I used to have a twin bed, so now I really appreciate the space of this bigger bed. I can sprawl out on it and not reach the edge. It's just sooo comfy!

Travis: I couldn't live without my radio. I like to listen to my music at all hours. I have to fall asleep with the radio playing.

Andrew: It's this soccer ball that's signed by Cobi Jones, who's a famous pro soccer player.

Tino: My model planes are my favorite things. I like to pick them up and look at them and study all the little details.

Chapter Three

Family Times

"When you spend time with your family, what do you usually do together?"

Lexy: We go out to dinner a lot. My family has a few favorite restaurants near where we live that we go to. Sometimes we rent videos and watch them together all smooshed on our big sofa. Usually we can't agree on one video, so sometimes we rent two and flip a coin to see which one we'll watch first. We'll pop a huge batch of popcorn and make a big deal out of it.

Devon: Our family hangs out playing with my baby brother. Since he's only 2 years old, it's hard to take him places where he won't get bored in a hurry and start screaming. (It's so embarrassing when he does that!) We hang around at home, or take him outside to goof around on the lawn or to play on his swingset or with his train. Sometimes we all go on little trips around the area — the park, public gardens, or museums.

Chrissy: My family likes to play board or card games. Especially on cold, snowy days when there isn't much to do, we sit on the living room rug and play games for hours.

Travis: We drive down to my grandparents' house because they live near the beach. We can ride our bikes all around, go visit the birds at this wildlife sanctuary by their house, and then eat dinner together. The kids sit at one table so we can really talk and have fun while the adults talk about boring things.

Andrew: My family and I go Rollerblading and bike-riding at the park near our house. We also go out to dinner a lot, which I really like.

Tino: We rent videos and gather in the living room to watch them. Sometimes we go to a park near our house and play baseball, ride bikes, or kick around a soccer ball. That's a lot of fun because everyone in the family just relaxes and has fun.

"What's your favorite together-time with your family?"

Lexy: I love it at Halloween when we go to this amusement park that they turn into a huge haunted house. It's so spooky but it's so much fun. They do so many things with special effects, it all seems so real. I get the shivers. It gets pretty crowded and everyone starts screaming. We go every year, and I look forward to it.

Devon: My favorite time is during the holidays when everyone slows down and we all huddle close together in the house. My big brother is home from school, so he takes me in his car and we go shopping together for presents. I really like when I get to help decorate the house with all the holiday things we have. It's fun to bake cookies with my brother. We make gingerbread cookies and decorate them with weird faces and hula skirts.

Chrissy: I like it best when we're all playing Uno. I'm pretty good at it, but even if I lose we all have so much fun.

Travis: My favorite time is when we all go to the beach together. Even in winter, sometimes we'll go at sunset and walk around the pier and buy something to eat.

Andrew: The time I like best is when we go to

the multiplex to catch a movie. We don't always agree on the movie, but even if we're watching one I really wasn't excited about seeing, I like being together with my family.

Tino: I like it best when we're all just talking together. We don't even have to be doing anything. Like when we just all happen to gather in the living room and everyone starts a big conversation and we start laughing, it's the best.

Karle: *What does family time mean to you? Do you have your own favorite times with your family?*

"What's the coolest thing about your parents?"

Lexy: The coolest thing about my parents is that they're willing to take me places I want to go even if it takes a long time to get there or it's a hassle. Sometimes I just wake up and get in the mood to go somewhere. We haven't planned anything for the day, and I'll say, "Could we go here?" out of the blue, and they usually just say, "Sure." I think that's pretty nice.

Devon: I think the coolest thing is that they trust me. Lots of parents always check up on their kids and treat them like they're up to something even when they're not. I really haven't done anything bad, so my parents know I'm not going to get into trouble. They let me go places without all of these nosy questions, and I really like that.

Chrissy: The coolest thing is they give me a big allowance. Of course, I can't spend it all. I have to put part in the church collection plate every week and part in the bank in my savings account. The rest I can spend how I please. I still have enough to buy some of the things I want.

Travis: They listen and understand me. They're willing to talk about all kinds of topics. They don't keep a bunch of things from me just because I'm a kid. I like it that they tell me funny stuff about their growing-up years. Sometimes we talk like regular friends, and I kinda forget they're my parents.

Andrew: They care about me and they don't yell at me that much. They could yell a lot more than they do, but they just quietly explain things and talk them out, which is what I like better.

Tino: They keep giving me more independence as I get older. I especially like it when they let me do things like go to the corner store on my own because it's not that close to my house.

"How do you get along with your siblings?"

Lexy: I get along really well with my sister. We do a lot of things together and share all kinds of secrets. It's a little different with my older brother. I love him, but since he's older, we don't get along as well. Sometimes he gets all annoyed when I'm singing or being silly, and that makes me mad. I mean, I'm just trying to have fun!

Devon: I'm very close to my brothers, so we don't argue much. My older brother is nice and takes me places in his car. We talk a lot about things I'm going through with my friends. He was in middle school once, and he knows how things happen, so he gives me advice. I get along with my baby brother too. He's fun to play with, and he's always so happy. That cheers me up when I've had a bad day. When I'm away from my little brother, I really miss him. Sometimes, though, I think people spoil him because he's a baby.

Chrissy: We get along pretty well. Sometimes we fight, though, like when I decide to go onto the computer, and my sister suddenly decides that she wants to go onto it. She'll come over and just shove me over. She'll start screaming that I'm hogging the computer, and my mom will tell me to be nice, that I'm the big sister. It makes me so mad! My sister is fun to play with, but when we travel a long way in the car together, we get on each other's nerves.

Travis: Sometimes my little brother and I quarrel. I'll play the games he wants to, and then when it's my turn, he gets all stubborn and won't play the games I want to. He knows since he's the youngest, he can make a huge fuss and everyone will think big brother is picking on him. My older brother and I are pretty different. Sometimes I get mad at him because he won't come outside and skateboard with me. Usually, we're both so busy with school and we don't seem to see each other that much, so we don't have time to hassle.

Andrew: We get along all right. Sometimes my older brother and I go at it. He can really make me annoyed, especially when he picks on me. I just want to beat him up at those times.

Tino: We get along pretty well. The only times we really fight are when my brother and sister won't play with me. Sometimes it doesn't seem like they're doing anything better, so I don't see why they won't do stuff with me.

* * *

"What do you wish to tell your parents but feel you can't?"

Lexy: I wish I could tell them that I'd like to redecorate my room, but the thing is, I just had it redecorated a couple of years ago. If I ask to redo it again, it might seem like I'm greedy. It's cute and all, but I've grown up a little and I've changed. I like different colors now, and I have all these new ideas for my room that I wish I could try.

Devon: Even though it's a long way away, I wish I could tell them that I'm scared to start high school. I don't sit there and obsess about it, but when I start to think about it, I get nervous. If I tell them, they'll just tell me that everything will be OK and all that kind of junk. It doesn't help that much, so I don't really bring it up.

Chrissy: I can tell them everything. They're easy to talk to, and even if I have a problem, I know they will understand and not yell at me. So why wouldn't I tell them everything?

Karle: *Lucky Chrissy!*

Travis: I wish I could tell them that I really think they should give me more privileges. I think I'm old enough to be given even more independence. Every time I try, they just think I'm looking for ways to get out of doing things I'm supposed to do.

Andrew: I usually tell them whatever's on my mind. I really don't hold anything back. I don't need to.

Tino: If I get into trouble at school, I want to tell them right away, but I don't feel I can. I don't want them to be mad at me.

* * *

"Do you have pets? If so, what kind?"

Lexy: I have a little hairy dog named Gilber. He's so cute and he follows us around the house. He sleeps in my room a lot.

Devon: My house is a zoo. We have four dogs: two huge Great Danes, a golden retriever, and a little white bichon, which is like a poodle. The bichon is named Heidi, and she is supposed to be my dog, but she always follows my mom around. We also have three cats, a dapple-gray Welsh pony named Maggie, and a fat guinea pig. We named him Mwoop because of the sound he makes when he's hungry.

Chrissy: I have two dogs and a guinea pig. The dogs are these really lovable old mutts named Boswick and Tootie. I like how happy they are to see me like when I come home from school. Tootie sleeps on my bed. My guinea pig is cute and cuddly, but I hate to clean his cage. It's so gross and it smells!

Travis: Our house is pretty full of animals, which I really like. I have a dalmatian named Spots, two cats, a chameleon named Pythagoras, and two rabbits.

Andrew: I have a Jack Russell terrier named Hercules. He's like a person, and he knows all these tricks. I had hamsters, but they died.

Tino: I have four cats — three kittens and their mother. I take care of them and I can spend hours playing with them and watching them wrestle with each other.

✲ ✲ ✲

"If you could have any pet, what would it be?"

Lexy: I'd have a hamster and some capybaras, which are these cute little furry rodent creatures. I think they're from South America. I've read about them in books and I think they'd be fun to have as pets.

> **Karle:** *Capybaras? They aren't cute — they're like huge rats!*

Devon: I've always wanted a manatee. They're so big and peaceful as they float around. I really like to watch them eat lettuce heads. They look like big dorks.

Karle: *Wow . . . talk about needing a really big fish tank! To keep a manatee as a pet she'd have to get a tank the size of a swimming pool!*

Chrissy: Any pet I don't have to take care of and clean up after.

Karle: *Ummm . . . that would be no pet I know of! Pets are definitely work.*

Travis: I'd do anything for a kangaroo. To me, it would be so much fun to have one hopping along beside you as you went down the street. I don't think I'd like to have one kick me or box me, though. That would probably really hurt!

Andrew: I'd like to have a golden retriever. Retrievers are pretty and loyal. They like to chase tennis balls, and I think one would make a good pet.

Tino: I want to have a Doberman pinscher. They're so smart and loyal. They look tough and cool.

Chapter Four

Friends

"Do you prefer to hang out with a best friend, or do you hang in a group?"

Lexy: I like to hang in big groups. It's more fun to do stuff with lots of friends at the same time. You can do so many more things and get more ideas when you're in a big group. Everyone has a different personality, so they all kind of mix together, which is more exciting than just being with one person. I have different moods so I like being with a whole bunch of buds at the same time.

Devon: There are times when having a best friend around is just right; and there are other times when I like being in a group. It just depends upon what I feel like at the time. I like being with one friend when we're just talking about something important that I don't want to share with the whole world. I like being in a big group when we're going somewhere, like the movies or camping or something. Then it's fun to have a lot of people to laugh and talk with.

Chrissy: I like being with my best friend the best. She and I are so close, and we do all kinds of fun things together that maybe other people wouldn't like to do. She understands me, and she always treats me like I'm special.

Travis: I like to hang with both. Sometimes it's fun to be with my best friend. I like to skateboard with him or hang. But when I go to a party, I want to be with all my friends. I like to talk with everyone and play games. The more the merrier.

Andrew: I like being in a big group best. I like being part of a team, doing something together. It's fun to hang with a big crowd at school, like at lunch. We always find stuff to laugh about.

Tino: I prefer to be with a best friend. I don't have to worry about so many people at once. Usually, my best friend and I agree on what we want to do, so it's easier than trying to find something that pleases a bunch of people at once. Sometimes that seems impossible!

Karle: ***Spending time with one best friend or hanging out with a group — both seem good! What's cool is just having friends to begin with!***

"Describe the qualities you look for in a best friend."

Lexy: I look for someone who isn't possessive. I hate having to worry if someone's mad because I'm talking with someone else or if I choose another girl to be my partner in, say, P.E. class when we have to pick a tennis partner. That causes some of the worst friendship problems, so it's better if I just hang with someone who's more like me. Also, I look for a person who isn't bossy and who's easygoing.

Devon: I look for someone with a sense of humor. I always like to joke around a lot because it helps keep me from being tense or bored, and it's fun if my friend likes to joke back. But they can't be mean jokes. I avoid people who say nasty things to others and then try to shrug it off by saying that it was just a joke. They're just looking for permission to be mean when they do that. I also look for a person who's creative and doesn't stab me in the back. I hate the kind of people who are nice to your face but do rude things behind your back. Then they come up to you the next minute. Like they think you didn't notice that they've just backstabbed you. They must be stupid to think you don't know what's really going on.

Chrissy: I look for someone who's understanding, funny, and loyal. I also look for someone who doesn't tease others.

Travis: I like a friendly, understanding person. It's important to me that my best friend gets along with other people, so there aren't always all these hassles. Also, if my friend is an understanding person, it'll be easier to talk about things and agree on places we'll go together.

Andrew: I look for someone who's nice, outgoing, and fun. Also, we have to have things in common.

Tino: I look for a person who's got a great personality, someone who's outgoing and nice to other people. I hate to be around people who rag on others, so my friend has to be caring and know how to treat others right.

✲ ✲ ✲

"When no one else is listening, what do you and your friends talk about?"

Lexy: Sometimes we talk about how mean others can be. It always surprises me that people do stuff to each other that they'd hate to have done to them. I just don't get it. It helps to talk about it with my friends so I can see that they're just as disgusted as I am about meanness.

Devon: We talk about feelings or we tell about our most embarrassing moments. We tell each other these stories, and we laugh about them; then they don't seem so horrible anymore. It kind of brings us together to see that we all have humiliating experiences, and it makes our friendships stronger.

Chrissy: I can't really say. It changes all the time. It kind of depends on the day, and whatever's going on at the moment. We talk about *everything*!

Travis: We talk mostly about stuff we want to do. Sometimes we talk about girls.

Andrew: We talk about sports. It depends what season it is, whether it's soccer, basketball, or baseball. We talk about the pro teams and players and who's got the best chances of going to the top.

Tino: We talk about movies and what we did that weekend. It's fun to compare what we did and find out what other people thought of a movie we've all seen.

Karle: *Hmmm . . . very interesting! The girls talk more about emotions and feelings while the boys discuss girls, sports, and movies! Wonder what that means? What about you and your friends? What do you talk about?*

"Where do you and your friends like to hang out?"

Lexy: We like to hang out on this big hill at school by the girls' locker room. It's got these shady trees on it, and it's away from all the noise of the other kids. We can talk and goof around without being interrupted. When we're at home, we go to each other's houses and that's really fun.

Devon: We like to hang together at the movies. We'll meet up early so that we can talk in front of the multiplex before the show starts. It's also fun to hang out at each other's houses. We like to go to different houses because each person has different stuff — one friend has a pool, another a tree house, and another a secret garden. It's nice to change the scenery when we hang out.

Chrissy: There's this big tree at our school and we all like to sit under it at lunch. It feels private and like we're in our own world, away from school and all the work.

Travis: We like to hang out in each other's rooms. It's fun to see each other's stuff and be in different places.

Andrew: We like to hang out at the movies. It's easy to get everyone to meet up when there's a good movie playing. Afterward, we can go to the little fast-food places around the cineplex and talk.

Tino: We like to hang out in this grassy area behind the school. Everyone just sort of drifts there after class, and we dump our books and backpacks and sprawl out. We relax and tell jokes before the bell rings and we have to go back to class.

Karle: ***Maybe boys and girls aren't that different after all — 'cause everyone likes hanging out with their friends!***

"Describe the absolute worst fight you ever had with a friend."

Lexy: The worst fight I had was when three of us were in the car, returning from a field trip, and we stopped for a submarine sandwich. To save money, two of us decided to share a turkey sandwich. The third girl got angry because she wanted ham, and she wanted to share a ham sandwich with me. It was nothing personal, but I just didn't feel like ham that day. I was mad that she'd be upset over such a stupid thing. We didn't speak to each other for the rest of the trip, and she stayed mad at me at school for a few days. We're still not that good friends because I can't really be close with someone who'll get that mad over something like that.

Devon: I think it was when my former best friend told someone else I copied the colors she wanted for her room when I had my room painted. It was so dumb because she was always talking about doing her room in every color of the rainbow, and she never redid her room anyway. If I stayed away from every color she said she wanted to do her room in, I couldn't have painted my room at all. I chose blue and yellow because I got a pretty new comforter and those colors looked perfect with it. I hated that she said such an unfair and mean thing while pretending to be my friend. We didn't exactly fight about it, but I was upset for a few days and cried a little because it hurt. We're not close anymore, partly because of that incident.

Chrissy: This girl didn't want me to be best friends with this other girl. She was so jealous, she called me the worst names and tried to turn my best friend against me. She really went out of her way to downtalk me and get this girl to be her friend, not mine. Luckily, it didn't work, and we're still best friends. It got so bad though, I wanted my mom to call her mom to make her stop. It was the worst!

Travis: There was this girl I was friends with. We used to be able to talk about everything, but we were just friends. One day, when I got a girlfriend, my girl bud suddenly got all weird and mad. She called crying and yelling at me and asking how I could do that to her. I was surprised that she'd think I wouldn't have time for her anymore. I got mad that she'd think I'd be such a bad friend that I'd just dump her because I now had a girlfriend. We didn't talk to each other for a few days, but finally I called her. We talked and I explained that she was important as a friend, so we worked it out.

Andrew: My friend and I were trying to decide what to do one day, and I wanted to play golf while he wanted to play hockey. Neither of us would budge, so we got into a heated argument. We finally decided to do both for part of the day, so it worked out. But for a while there, whew! It was tense.

Tino: Every day at lunch hour, my buddy and I play soccer or kickball together. Then this one day, my buddy started kicking around a ball with this other guy. I wanted to play too, and they ignored me. They would kick the ball around me, and when I'd run for it, they'd dart ahead of me and take it away. I started yelling at my friend and asking why I couldn't jump in. He just cut me dead and pretended not to hear me. I was so angry I wanted to slug him, but I just walked away. Later he apologized and said he just didn't feel like making it a three-way game at the time. I was still mad, but I let it go. It wasn't worth wrecking a friendship over.

Karle: ***The boys seem to be able to patch things up and move on while the girls . . . well, seems like they find forgiving and forgetting a little harder to do. How is it with you and your friends?***

"If you saw a friend cheating on a test, what would you do?"

Lexy: My friends wouldn't cheat, but if I saw someone cheating, I wouldn't say anything right then, but later I'd really let them have it. I'd ask why they felt they had to go that low. It's much easier to study and not risk getting caught.

Devon: I'd wait till afterward to say anything. If I were to say something right then and there, the teacher might think I was the one whispering and cheating. I'd walk up to them in the hall after the test was over, tell them I saw it and that they shouldn't do that. I think it'd make me feel weird about that person for a long time because cheating's a pretty bad thing.

Chrissy: I'd tell her to stop right there, or I'd tell the teacher. And I wouldn't be afraid to do it, either. I don't think it's fair to the other kids who aren't cheating. They work hard.

Travis: I'd wait till after the test or whatever, pull that person aside, and say that it made me think less of him or her. I mean, it's better to flunk a test than drag your reputation in the mud.

Andrew: I wouldn't hold back. I'd whisper to that person to knock it off. Cheating makes me mad. I mean, everyone else has to do the work. Why shouldn't that kid?

Tino: I'd put my eyes back on my paper because I wouldn't want to be accused of cheating too. Later, I'd ask the person why he cheated. Cheating's wrong. I hate it when someone gets away with it and brags about what a great grade he got.

> **Karle:** *It's cool that both the girls and boys realize how wrong cheating is and won't put up with it!*

"If you saw a friend teasing someone, what would you do?"

Lexy: That's an easy question. It makes me so mad when people tease others. I'd just tell them to stop right then and there.

Devon: I'm not shy when it comes to that kind

of thing. I'd stand up for that person and get the teaser to stop it.

Chrissy: I'd stick up for the person who was being teased because I know what it's like to be teased. It's just plain mean.

Travis: I'd tell the person to cool it. I remember what it was like before I had lots of friends. People would tease me when I first came to my new school, and I hated it. I'd let the person know how mean and childish I thought it was to pick on someone else.

Andrew: I'd tell the person that others have feelings too and try to get them to stop what they were doing.

Tino: I'd tell them to stop in a loud voice so that others would hear it too and the person would be embarrassed about what he was doing. That's the best way to get someone to stop.

Karle: ***Well, alright! Standing up for kids getting teased and trying to stop it is way cool!***

"In your opinion, what is it that people like about you?"

Lexy: I think people like the way I never get all cranky outwardly. Even if I'm mad about something, I don't think everyone else should have to suffer. I try not to take my bad moods out on others. I just keep smiling and try to work out whatever's bothering me until I get over it.

Devon: I think people like that I'm consistently kind and that I try to make bad things seem better by using humor. I think people can count on me because they know that I don't change.

Chrissy: I think they like my loyalty. I defend my friends and always stand by them. People appreciate it when you're like that.

Travis: I think that people like that I am my own person; I don't change my opinions because everyone else feels another way.

Andrew: I'm nice and funny, so I think it's easy to be around me. People like to laugh when they're worried about something and they know around me they won't be worried for long.

Tino: I think people like my sense of humor. I like to tell jokes and my friends like to hear them.

Karle: ***A sense of humor is definitely a great thing to have. What about you? Do you make people laugh?***

"What do you wish you could tell your best friend but feel you can't?"

Lexy: I'd like to tell her I like the same boy she does. She talks about him a lot, and I think she'd hate it if she knew that I liked him too. I never say anything. It's not worth causing a problem.

Devon: I'd like to tell my friend that sometimes she wears too much jewelry. Like we'll be playing a sport, and she'll come into the gym clanking with all these bracelets. She looks like she's trying too hard to impress, and why does she want to impress a bunch of sweaty gym rats anyway?

Chrissy: I can tell her anything. She's easy to talk to and she never teases me even when I tell her something she could tease me about.

Karle: ***How lucky to have a best bud like that!***

Travis: I can tell him anything. That's kind of the point of a best friend. I mean, it's other people you have to watch what you say with.

Andrew: Sometimes my friend gets a bad haircut, and I don't say anything, but I'd like to tell him to try another type of cut. It looks so weird. But I pretend not to notice so I don't hurt his feelings.

Tino: I'd like to tell him when a girl tells me she likes him but not to let him know. It would be fun to let my buddy know that someone likes him, especially if he likes her. Thing is, though, if I tell someone I won't tell, then I don't tell. That's why people trust me.

* * *

"Is it easy to have a guy friend? Why or why not?" (We only asked the girls.)

Lexy: Not really. Guys aren't that easy to talk to. They have a different way of looking at things, so you don't exactly feel safe saying stuff around them. You never know how they'll take something, and you'll end up feeling like a geek! Anyway, some guys are mean to girls or they do things that are so gross, you really don't want to be their friend.

Devon: I have a few guy friends. I'm starting to have more because I'm starting to understand how to talk to them. I used to treat them different because they were guys, but now I realize they're people just like girls are. (I know, duh! But it took a while to realize that.) Now I talk with them and don't worry so much about what I'm saying. I figure that they like it when a girl makes the effort.

Chrissy: I have a few guy friends. It helps to know a guy for a long time. Like this guy who lives across the street from me, we've known each other since we were babies. We hang at each other's houses, and I don't get all weird thinking he's a guy or anything. He's a friend, and we can talk about most stuff.

"Is it easy to have a girl pal? Why or why not?" (We only asked the boys.)

Travis: I have a zillion girl buddies. They're easy to make friends with and easy to talk to. Sometimes they're easier to talk to than guys. It's fun when they come to me with their problems about guys, because I can help them. Sometimes I don't understand them, though, when they fight with their friends.

Andrew: I have a few girl pals. I don't know if they're easier or harder to be friends with than guys. I just make friends with the ones who are nice and have good personalities, and I don't really think about it more than that.

Tino: I have a few girl buddies. Usually the girls play soccer with us at school. We can talk about soccer and things we're all interested in, so it's easier to start conversations with them than with girls I don't have anything in common with.

Karle: *Guys and girls sometimes have a few problems when it comes to being friends. See chapter six.*

Chapter Five

Class Act

"Is there a popular crowd at your school?"

Lexy: There definitely is a popular crowd at our school. A lot of boys and girls belong to it, and our class isn't that big. The kids in this crowd sit together and do stuff with each other after school. They get all excited about what girl likes what boy and who broke up with who. It's kind of funny. They think they have all this power and that they rule, but other people like hanging with their own friends and aren't jealous or anything.

Devon: There is a popular crowd at my school, but it was more of a big deal a couple of years ago than it is now. I guess the popular people realized they were missing something by closing themselves off and now the walls dividing everyone have sort of come down. There are some kids who think they're better than everyone else, but they're the only ones who think so.

Chrissy: There really isn't a popular crowd at my school. Most kids hang together in small groups of two or three. Maybe some people are better at making friends than others, but there isn't really one group that's more of a big deal than another.

Travis: There's a huge popular crowd at my school. These kids are kind of the trendsetters. They start to wear something or do something, and the other kids copy it. They walk around school in big groups and get together outside of school. They're sort of the leaders and get elected to the clubs and things because everyone knows them. They're pretty nice, though, and usually only don't like others if those kids are mean to people.

Andrew: There is a popular crowd at our school, I guess, but it's not that set apart from the rest of the kids the way it is in other places. Most everyone kind of hangs together and drifts in and out of smaller groups.

Tino: There isn't a popular crowd at our school. Everyone just kind of hangs with their own friends. No one is really considered more popular than someone else. It's all kind of equal.

Karle: ***What's the deal at your school? Does the popular crowd rule — or is there room for everyone?***

"How do you get to be in the popular crowd?"

Lexy: You hang out with the popular kids, and you don't say much at first. Like you don't disagree too strongly — you just kind of quietly fit in. You go slowly and make friends with them, and then you're in!

Devon: You wear certain kinds of clothes and you laugh at anything they say, even if it's not funny. Oh, yeah, you always have to pretend you're having fun. I think it's kind of weird. These people stuff down who they really are so they can join in this big blob of everyone who acts and thinks alike.

Chrissy: Since there really isn't a popular crowd at my school, I couldn't tell you.

Travis: Well you have to dress right for one thing. It shouldn't matter what you wear, I guess. But to some people it does. Like at our school, the cool kids wear skater kinds of clothes. The girls wear these brand-name T-shirts or blouses and whatever style of pants that are in. But really, it's most important to be nice and know how to have fun. If you start to tease any member of the group, you will find yourself edged out, which I think is a good thing. That means people are pretty loyal.

Andrew: You have to have nicer clothes and shoes. The shoes have to be the newest styles and the clothes are certain types. If there's a cool kind of shirt, the popular kids have lots of them. I think people are careful to wear the clothes that everyone else considers cool.

Tino: I can't answer that question because we don't have crowds like that at our school.

Karle: *Do these comments sound familiar? What is the popular crowd at your school like?*

"What is your favorite subject in school? Why?"

Lexy: I absolutely love art. It's not academic, so there aren't all these rules. Nothing's right or wrong. It's all about how you want to express yourself. You get to be free and do whatever you want. That's why I like it. I like to create things and use my imagination. When I'm painting, the class hour flies by, which is so different than some other classes that seem to drag on and on.

Devon: My favorite subject is science. It's easy to understand and it explains why things are the way they are. My teacher this year is so knowledgeable. He's smart and he's traveled around the world on a sailboat. You know he knows what he's talking about. He never has to fake like he knows something when he doesn't, like other teachers. You can ask him anything, and he can answer it in a way that's so interesting.

Chrissy: I love math. It's so easy and fun. The problems are kind of like puzzles or games to me. And since I like games, I guess that's why I like math. Sometimes it can be hard, but that's maybe why it's so interesting because you really have to think. I think it's sad when people don't like math because I think they're missing out on something fun.

Travis: I like world history because I'm pretty interested in how people made decisions in the past, considering what they knew then. I like to think about which were good and which were bad decisions. Also, I like to figure out why some people are dorks today and follow in the footsteps of bad leaders and make the same mistakes. It all ends up being another big mess just like it was in historical times. You'd think people would learn, but nooooo!

Andrew: I like math and social studies. I think math is easy and so I'm pretty good at it. Also, I like social studies because I really want to know about the past. Some historical times were more interesting than times are today.

Tino: My favorite subject is history. I particularly like learning about World War II because I'm so into aviation and the fighter planes that were used in the war. The other periods of history are OK, but when we get to World War II, I find I'm more interested and it's easier to do all the reading.

Karle: *Wow! No one even said gym or P.E.!*

"Which subject is it that you totally can't stand?"

Lexy: I hate history. It's pointless; I mean it's over. What's done is done. You can't change it or anything, so I don't see why we have to spend so much time having to learn it.

Devon: I don't like history. I used to love it, but last year, we had the worst teacher. He was a huge bore, and I grew to hate the whole subject. He blabbed on and on and everyone fell asleep in his class. Anyway, history is a hard subject because you have to remember all these meaningless dates. The textbooks are boring because they're so simplified. They're full of names and dates, and they don't really get in there and give you details that tell you why something happened. That would make it interesting.

Chrissy: Health class is the worst. It's sooo boring. I get so tired when I'm in that class. The teacher just goes on and on telling you all this junk you already know. It seems preachy, like you're always being lectured — "Do this, don't do that."

Travis: I don't like English. It's so tedious. I hate walking into that class. You have to write paragraphs, which take sooo long. I really can't think of anything to write about. It would be much easier to just talk about it. I especially hate learning parts of speech. I don't get it. It seems like the only reason you do that is to prove you know it. There's no other reason to know whether a word is an adjective, verb, or noun. I think you can live your whole life fine without knowing grammar.

Andrew: Yuck. Language arts is the one I hate. You do all these drills. Start, stop. Start, stop. I like to just go on and do something until it's finished. Also language arts requires all of these dumb assignments.

Tino: I don't like math. It's too hard and makes my head ache. I don't like how you have to do problem after problem of the same kind. Why not just do one or two? By then you know if you can do it or not — without going through all the hassle.

Karle: *One person's favorite subject is another's worst nightmare. Like math and history — either you love it or you hate it. Where do you stand?*

"How long does it take you to get ready for school in the morning?"

Lexy: It takes me about a half hour. I shower, jump into my clothes, and brush my hair. That's it.

Devon: It takes me an hour. Everyone complains that I take long showers, but that's how I wake up. I spend time styling my hair because I like to change the way I wear it a lot. Good thing I have a uniform for school. It's pretty ugly because it's a sick yellow-green. Still, if I didn't have to wear it, I think I would take lots of time trying to decide what to wear in the morning.

Chrissy: It takes me about 30 to 45 minutes. My mom says I go kind of slow, but I don't think I do. I just like to think about what I wear and go through what I do without forgetting to do part of it because I'm being rushed. I hate getting to school and realizing I forgot something.

Travis: It depends. If I wake up late, I can zoom out the door in about five minutes. If I have time, it'll take me about 15 minutes, including the time I take to feed my animals. Feeding my animals takes most of my time getting ready because I have so many.

Andrew: It takes me about 20 minutes to shower, get dressed, and eat.

Tino: It takes me 15 minutes.

Karle: ***Boys sure are quick in the morning — they are up and out in no time!***

"Do you eat breakfast? If so, what do you eat?"

Lexy: I eat breakfast every day. Usually, my mom makes us eggs and bacon with cereal, and sometimes she makes chocolate chip pancakes. I love those.

Devon: I wolf down a bowl of cereal and usually some fruit. Sometimes I want to skip it, like if I'm late, but then I know my stomach will be all growly by late morning and I won't be able to concentrate in class. I'll have food on the brain instead.

Chrissy: I have cereal or these strudel thingies. There really isn't time to make a huge deal out of breakfast.

Travis: I almost always eat cereal. It's the fastest thing. I just scarf it down and bolt out the door.

Andrew: I eat cereal or if there's not much time, a muffin.

Tino: I usually have pancakes or waffles. I'm usually pretty hungry in the morning and it seems like a long time until lunch.

* * *

"Do you consider yourself to be a good student?"

Lexy: I'm a pretty good student. I work hard and study a lot. My grades are important to me, and it helps to always know I'm doing my best.

Devon: I'm a good student. I take my homework seriously and try to do the extra credit whenever I can. I like to be precise and do as good a job as I can. Sometimes when I have a lot to do, it's really hard because I don't want to breeze through one of the assignments so I can get to the next one. Even if I'm really tired, I try to stay up and do the work the way it's supposed to be done.

Chrissy: I'm a pretty good student. I work hard on my homework and lots of times I get my dad to look it over afterward to make sure I've done it right. I make sure to copy all my assignments into my homework notebook so I don't forget anything.

Travis: I'm an OK student. Sometimes I wish I were better. I sometimes blast through an assignment just to get it done. There are just so many other interesting things to do after school. I figure I'm in school all day, so the afternoons shouldn't have to be filled with a ton of schoolwork. I don't like it when I get low grades.

Andrew: I'm a good student. I work hard and try to get all my work in on time.

Tino: I'm a good student. I do a lot of reading and that helps.

"If you could say one thing to your teacher, what would it be?"

Lexy: One of my teachers has this horrible goatee. He just grew it last year. It looks stupid and I can hardly look at him without thinking about it. I'd like to tell him to get rid of it!

Devon: I'd have liked to tell my history teacher that he definitely is the worst teacher I've ever had — and that he ought to find a different job. It made me mad that every day he wasted my time and made me and my friends hate history.

Chrissy: I pretty much tell my teachers what's on my mind. I guess, though, there was that time when I wished I could tell one teacher that I didn't do something that she thought I did.

Travis: I'd like to disagree instead of having to go along with stupid things that they say. If you try to tell a teacher you disagree, they think you're disrepecting them, so you have to be careful and not say anything.

Andrew: I'd like to tell all of them not to give so many assignments. It's like they try to jam so much in and it's not like you learn all that much doing them.

Tino: I'd like to tell some of my teachers to be nicer. Some of them think the only way they can be the boss is to be jerks and get really down on their students. Also, teachers don't need to yell so much. I'd like to tell them that kids are trying most of the time, and the teachers can be so impatient.

Karle: ***Do you think teachers would be surprised by these comments?***

"What's the biggest problem at your school?"

Lexy: The way I see it, the biggest problem is that there are all these little cliques. Everyone has to join one, and they don't get along with the other ones. I think it would be more fun if people could sit with different people at lunch or whatever. You'd hear new things and it would be more interesting. I'd like to be friends with people outside my group too.

Devon: I think our biggest problem is that a lot of kids at the school are competitive about everything. You can't buy a cute shirt without someone having to go out and get two of them. If you tell a story at the lunch table, so many people try to top it. Everyone goes out for every sports team and wants to beat your pants off. They would do anything to get a better grade on a test than another person. People cry when they don't make things. It takes away a lot of the fun of going for stuff. You feel bad if you don't make it, and you feel bad if you make a team and one of your friends doesn't.

Chrissy: People at our school write notes with bad words on them and pass them around class. Also, some of them use really disgusting language everywhere — in the halls and on the playground. I don't see why they have to do that. They can say what they mean without having to get all dirty about it.

Travis: I think it's that people's opinions are too strong. They believe they're right no matter what and try to force others to think like they do. I think there's room for people to have different opinions. It kind of makes people think twice about saying something because they don't want to start arguments, and I think that's sad.

Andrew: There are fights all the time. They break out by the lockers or out on the fields and everyone crowds around to watch. Most of the time they're about the dumbest things and aren't worth hurting someone over. Talk about stupid!

Tino: I think it's the way so many kids trash the campus. They toss their litter everywhere and leave food on the tables. It's disrespectful to be so messy and it makes school so dirty all the time. I think everyone would feel more proud if they took better care not to litter.

"What are your favorite activities in gym class?"

Lexy: I like when we do gymnastics. Gymnastics can be sort of like dance, and it's artistic as well. I think it's fun to tumble and try new moves. We don't get to do it often enough, however.

Devon: I like when we play any team sport and are practicing together. It doesn't matter what it is. When we do it day after day and you start to see everyone get better, I think that's the best part. I like learning new skills when it comes to a game I've been playing a long time.

Chrissy: We get to ride on these little scooters sometimes. We have these stations in the gym and you move around to different ones. One of them is the scooter station. I like whipping around on the scooters and laughing with my friends. The time at that station goes so quickly, and you never get enough turns. I also like basketball. I like shooting and trying to score points.

Travis: I like baseball and track events. I like baseball because I'm a pretty good hitter. Track's fun too because there aren't all these rules and there's a clear-cut winner. You just have to watch and see who runs the fastest.

Andrew: What else? Soccer. I guess it's because I've played all these years and am pretty good at it. I feel good stepping out onto the field and knowing that I'll do well because I've got a lot of experience. But I also like hockey.

Tino: I like soccer and kickball. It's cool to get out there and just punch a ball with your foot and run around. I like being on a team and trying to beat the opponent.

Chapter Six

Girl Talk, Guy Talk

"In your opinion, what's the weirdest thing about boys?" (We only asked the girls.)

Lexy: I don't understand why they're so into blood, guts, and gore. I mean, the movies they like are all these scary and bloody ones. I also think it's weird the way they get all interested in gross stuff in science class. One minute they're asleep, and then the teacher shows some really *ugh* thing, and they wake right up and become all into it. I just don't get it.

Devon: I think it's weird how they follow one or two really bad guys around like puppies and try to show off for them by doing bad stuff too. It seems like they don't use their own minds to decide that that's wrong. They're the ones who get into trouble, and they go right back and do it again to impress some loser. They're so busy trying to act cool.

Chrissy: The weirdest thing is that they spit — anywhere and everywhere. Girls never do that, but guys do it all the time without thinking twice about it. Everyone else is so disgusted, and the guys who do it are not even the least little bit embarrassed about it! Eeeew!

* * *

"In your opinion, what's the weirdest thing about girls?"
(We only asked the boys.)

Travis: It's weird the way they become so serious about some little thing. They'll take a little forgettable comment someone makes and turn it into a huge deal and obsess about it for days. They'll call you up and talk and talk about it, and you don't really even remember what it was all about. Don't ask me why!

Andrew: I think it's strange the way they worry so much — about everything. Their hair, their clothes, their shoes. It's like they're so picky about all these unimportant details.

Tino: I think it's weird the way some girls hit and kick and slap people, like shove them out of the way in a crowded hallway or whatever.

Karle: ***Do you think the boys' comments are fair or are they exaggerated?***

"What do you wish you had or could do that boys have or can do?" (We only asked the girls.)

Lexy: There's nothing. I can do anything they can do. When it comes to sports, we can play any game that they can. In class, we can be as good as they are. They don't really have any advantages.

Devon: There isn't anything they have or do that I'd want. Maybe in the old days guys could do some things that girls couldn't do. But that's not true anymore. If a girl wants to participate in something, even football, she can just do it. No one really thinks about it.

Chrissy: Guys don't ever have to wear dresses, and I wish girls didn't ever have to. It's not like I have to wear one all the time, but when I'm forced to put one on, I am so jealous of guys.

"What do you wish you had or could do that girls have or can do?" (We only asked the boys.)

Travis: I wish guys got second chances the way girls do. Guys usually get only one shot, and they get into trouble. Like at school, if a girl is goofing around, the teacher will usually just say, "If you do that one more time . . . " Whereas for a guy, they'll send him to the office right then and there.

Karle: *Do you think that's really the way it is?*

Andrew: I can't think of any advantage they have.

Tino: There isn't anything.

Karle: *That's cool. Guys and girls seem to be able to choose what they want to do and not be cornered into something just because "girls are supposed to" or "guys are supposed to."*

"What do you think about what boys wear?" (We only asked the girls.)

Lexy: They dress weird. I mean, what's the big deal about wearing your boxers above your pants? No one wants to see boxers. Guys have to be uncomfortable always tugging their pants and sagging them but being careful they don't fall down. I think it looks, well, bizarre!

Devon: Their clothes are pretty plain. They don't have as many choices of styles or colors as girls. Anyway, they don't try new things. They just do the baggy thing because their friends all do it. Boh-ring!

Chrissy: I think it's funny how cool they think they look in their clothes, and to me they're just blah. They don't have choices like girls.

"What do you think about what girls wear?"
(We only asked the boys.)

Travis: Their clothes are all right, but they worry so much about looking perfect all the time. It's like it's the end of the world if they get a spot on one of their outfits. Clothes are just . . . clothes.

Andrew: I don't really notice what they wear all that much. I do notice that they're so picky and make a huge deal about clothes, which I think is a waste of time. They freak out if they get a stain. Well, big deal! It'll wash out and if it doesn't, they'll probably get a new shirt that they like even more.

Tino: I think girls dress so strangely sometimes, like when they try too hard to be trendy and wear, say, one yellow and one blue sock to match their outfit. It doesn't look cool, it just looks dumb.

Karle: *It's unanimous — the boys don't get girls' fashions and the girls don't understand why boys dress the way they do, either!*

"Complete the sentence: I wish more girls would . . ."

Lexy: . . . stand up to boys. When guys tease them or push them around, most girls kind of shrink back and look for ways to avoid them instead of just getting in their face and telling them to stop — NOW.

Devon: . . . be more confident. They can be so insecure and worry so much about what other people think of them. They copy other's clothes instead of developing their own style.

Chrissy: . . . be nicer to each other. Girls can really pick on other girls, and I think they ought to stick together.

Travis: . . . get along with each other. They miss out on having more friends because they're always so jealous of each other.

Andrew: . . . be nicer to each other. I can't believe how mean some girls are to others. And it doesn't seem like there's ever really a good reason.

Tino: . . . be nicer to me.

Karle: ***Do you also think girls need to lighten up?***

"Complete the sentence: I wish more guys would . . ."

Lexy: . . . be more sensitive. Sometimes they say or do the meanest things without taking a second to think about how much those things can hurt someone.

Devon: . . . express their feelings. You can't tell what's on their minds, and it would be much simpler if you knew. It could save a lot of misunderstandings and arguments.

Chrissy: . . . stop being so bossy. It's really not necessary and it just makes you dislike them.

Travis: . . . not be determined to get you to think like they do. It's like theirs is the only opinion that matters in the whole world.

Andrew: . . . not brag. They just seem stupid and no one is impressed that they own this or that or that they can do something better than someone else. It could all change tomorrow.

Tino: . . . stop hitting little kids. I see it all the time at school and around where I live. They just look for smaller and weaker people and pound on them.

Karle: ***Do you think boys need to do something about their attitudes?***

"Complete the sentence: I wish more girls wouldn't . . ."

Lexy: . . . be so crazy about makeup and hair. It used to be more fun when the girls I knew weren't so into their looks. It just makes you worried about how you look all the time, and I hate it. Besides, it can be so boring talking about hairstyles and what color lip gloss you should wear.

Devon: . . . worry about clothes so much. Sometimes people I know start talking about shopping and what they thought was sooo cute or sooo ugly, and I want to scream. I'd rather talk about interesting stuff.

Chrissy: . . . be so hard on others. Girls should stick up for each other and not always look for stuff to tease them about. There are enough problems in the world without people trying to make it worse.

Travis: . . . try to rope others into their fights and try to get everyone to hate someone just because they're fighting with that person.

Andrew: . . . be so intense about their clothes because no one else really cares.

Tino: . . . push other kids around. They ought to just be more respectful of others and not always want to pound on people.

"Complete the sentence: I wish more guys wouldn't . . ."

Lexy: . . . act all tough and macho. Everyone knows they're not really like that inside, so it would be much more fun if they'd just be real and let people get to know who they really are.

Devon: . . . try so hard to be liked by the so-called cool kids that they get themselves into trouble.

Chrissy: . . . tease girls so much. Leave us alone!

Travis: . . . be jerks to each other.

Andrew: . . . be mean to littler kids. I hate to see older guys beating up on little guys just because they're bigger. It's unfair.

Tino: . . . do bad stuff. You could relax more if you didn't have to worry about what some guys were going to do next.

Karle: *So girls can be superficial and boys can be bullies? Do you think this is true?*

"What's the best thing about being a girl?" (We only asked the girls.)

Lexy: I think the best part is that girls can do anything without being ridiculed for it—play army or play with dolls. I mean, if a boy takes ballet or something, he would be totally teased forever.

Devon: I like how we can wear our hair in a million styles and we can wear all kinds of clothes — outdoorsy, sporty, or girly. Boys don't have many choices. Like if you're a boy, and you don't like spiked or buzzed hair, you're out of luck.

Chrissy: We can wear our hair in all kinds of different styles.

*****

"What's the best thing about being a boy?" (We only asked the boys.)

Travis: I like being able to ask out a girl instead of waiting to be asked out. I mean, girls can ask out guys, but it's not the same.

Andrew: I like the fact that we're generally better at sports. I mean, women's and men's sports just aren't the same.

Tino: I like that most guys are better at athletics.

> **Karle:** ***Guys are better athletes? Don't you think all the athletic girls and women out there prove them wrong?***

"What makes a girl cute?"

Lexy: I think it's mostly her face. If she smiles

a lot and her eyes are happy. After that, it's her clothes, but clothes aren't as important.

Devon: A girl who's cute usually smiles easily and seems to be self-confident. It also helps if she has her own sense of style.

Chrissy: I look at a girl and think she's cute if she wears her hair in a way that shows she knows how to have fun. I mean, it doesn't always work. But for the most part, if she's wearing a French braid or a bouncy ponytail, you know she's active and likes to do things. That makes her cute!

Travis: I think what makes a girl cute is if she has a good appearance, like she takes care of herself. She thinks about what she wears — but not too much. A girl can have a pretty face, but if she's not nice and understanding, she's just not cute.

Andrew: I think it's important to have a nice smile. After that, a nice face is part of the overall cute thing.

Tino: A girl is cute to me if she's got a happy face.

Karle: *Seems like a big smile goes a long way toward upping a girl's cute quotient!*

"What makes a boy cool?"

Lexy: Cool guys are the ones who make an

effort to be friends with girls, who know how to treat others right. If they're mean, no matter how wonderful they think they are, they're not cool.

Devon: To me, a guy is cool if he is confident, but not overboard so that he's arrogant and brags all the time. It helps if he has a sense of humor to keep things light.

Chrissy: A guy who's cool is one who knows how to be nice to people. He's cool if he can sit on the bus and not tease girls just to be mean.

Travis: A guy is cool if he knows who he is and doesn't seem to be trying to figure that out all the time by following others.

Andrew: I think guys who know how to dress well are cool. Also guys who are good on the sports field but know how to win and lose with good sportsmanship are pretty cool.

Tino: I think cool guys are the ones who are comfortable with who they are and don't have to do bad stuff to prove how cool they are. You can just tell by looking at them that they know who they are and that they're not about to change to try to impress you.

Karle: ***Seems like cool isn't about what you look like, but how you treat people. That is cool.***

Chapter Seven

Sports Watch

"What's your favorite sport to watch?"

Lexy: I really like to watch women's soccer, probably because I play and really understand it. The games are never boring. They go so fast. I like to see the teamwork. It's best to watch it on TV so you can see the plays develop.

Devon: I like pro soccer. Men's or women's, it doesn't matter. It's cool to see their formations and the incredible stops pro goalies make.

Chrissy: I like to watch basketball. I used to like watching Michael Jordan play, and I like to watch Scottie Pippin. I guess you can tell I'm a Bulls fan!

Travis: I like watching major-league baseball. The pro players make everything seem so easy, and it's fun to watch people breaking records.

Andrew: I like watching soccer. I especially

like the teams from France. They're so good and exciting. You never know what they'll do next.

Tino: Soccer's definitely my favorite. Whenever there's a game on TV, I like to watch it. I also like going to see the games at the stadium if I can get my dad to take me. My sister plays on a rec-league team, and I even like to go watch her games because I just love the sport.

Karle: *Guess there are a lot of soccer fans out there — boys and girls!*

"What's your favorite sport to play?"

Lexy: Definitely soccer.

Devon: I can't name a favorite. I play softball, soccer, and volleyball and I absolutely love them all. It's nice to win, but it's not that bad to lose when you have nice girls on your team, and you're all cheering for each other. It's nice to travel together to tournaments and sing goofy songs and talk about strategies.

Chrissy: I like playing softball. I play all kinds of positions, but especially outfield because I'm pretty good at catching fly balls. It's fun to cheer on a teammate when she's up at bat.

Travis: Baseball. I play on a senior Little League team, and each year I can't wait until opening day. I like hitting, and I go to the batting cage to try to get better.

Andrew: Soccer. I've been playing for years, and have been to so many tournaments. I like it when the level of competition's good. It's not that much fun when you beat the same team a bunch of times. It's just too easy.

Tino: Football. I like getting out there, and getting the ball and having people try to tackle me. I try to run fast so no one can catch me.

"Do you prefer to play coed or noncoed sports?"

Lexy: I prefer noncoed sports. When you play coed sports, the guys tend to hog the ball and act like the girls aren't even on the field. When girls play together, you know what to expect. I think girls are better team players than guys are. Each guy likes to think he's the best.

Devon: I like noncoed. We really never play coed sports except once in a while in P.E. Boys and girls play two totally different types of games. For example, in soccer, girls tend to pass more, where guys run with the ball, so it's confusing, and you can't play the way you normally play. Sometimes one guy is flirting with one girl, so in basketball, he'll try to dish off to her when she's not even open. When people do that, the level of competition goes down and it's not that much fun.

Chrissy: I like coed sports. Having boys on the playing field makes the girls try harder to outdo the guys and sparks the game along.

Travis: I like noncoed sports. If you're playing lawn football with girls, you can't tackle so hard. It's not as much fun if you have to hold back. Yeah, some girls play tough, but if you hurt a girl, you feel bad and everyone thinks you're a bully.

Andrew: I like noncoed sports. Whenever you play coed sports, you can't be as competitive because it's supposed to be a more social type of thing, so the game isn't as much fun.

Tino: I like coed sports. You tend to goof around more, so it's not so much about winning. You laugh more and have more fun.

Conclusion

Take a Chance

So there you have it: the real deal on six kids like you. Could you see these kids as your friends and, if you were to meet them, would you be outgoing around them or shy?

It's not always easy at first; sometimes you've just got to take the risk and throw out a few friendly questions. Sure, you might have to get your guts up and be brave, but it could be worth it if you can spark a friendship and learn more about others with whom you share the planet!